THANK YOU FOR PARTNERING
WITH US TO BUILD YOUR
BRIDGE.

Ethan

LIFE'S BRIDGES

LIFE'S BRIDGES
Building Your Bridge to Financial Wealth

Lloyd Lowe Sr. and Ethan Bonar

LIFE'S BRIDGES
Building Your Bridge to Financial Wealth

For information, please contact:
Brown Books Publishing Grouop
16200 North Dallas Parkway, Suite 170
Dallas, Texas 75248

www.brownbooks.com
972-381-0009
A New Era in Publishing™

ISBN-13: 978-1-934812-58-7
ISBN-10: 1-934812-58-7
LCCN:2009941271

Contents

Introduction

If you have a vision of what you want your future to be, I believe this book can help you achieve it. Like any journey, the journey to your financial future begins with a single step. To build the bridge to your financial future, you have to make the decision to take that first step. Once you make that decision, and once you have a blueprint for how you are going to build your bridge, your odds of enriching your financial future are better than ever before.

As a financial advisor who has helped people from all walks of life prepare for their future, I have come to understand that every investor has their own vision of what they want that to be. I also understand that vision is just that—your vision, not mine—and that each investor's vision is as unique and as individual as they are. As we like to say in our firm, "If you can dream it, we can create a custom plan to help you attain it." I think this book, along with qualified advice from a trained, tenured financial advisor, can help you attain your dream, whatever it is.

Now, build your personal bridge to the lifestyle you want.

–Lloyd Lowe Sr.

Chapter 1

Building the Bridge to Your Financial Future

When it comes to financial planning and your long-term financial future, you need a well-constructed bridge to get from here to success. To build that bridge, you will need goals and a plan to reach them.

How Do You Define "Happily Ever After"?

When most people think of planning for the future, they think of retirement.

To many people, retirement seems a long way off, something you only do when you have grown too old to do anything else. I would like to suggest thinking of retirement in a different way. Try thinking of it as a bridge to the things that you do not have time for while working—travel, start a business, pursue a hobby, engage in charitable work, go back to school, be closer to family, or simply relax. Because retirement is such an important phase in your life—and because you only get one real chance to do it right—careful planning is a must.

But planning is not just something that is nice to do if you can find the time. It is something that you will most likely find essential sooner or later. Here is another way to think of it: you will need to have money in retirement, and if you do not plan on working in retirement, where will this money come from? It is a fact that, unfortunately, many people never really think this through. However, proper retirement planning will answer all of these questions before you retire.

What Is Your Retirement Scenario?

Most people assume three sources of income will work together to fund retirement: Social Security, pensions, and personal savings. Even with these three possible income streams, there are still problems to consider.

First, there is no way to be certain about what the future holds for Social Security. Even if the best-case scenario works out and you receive full Social Security benefits, the average person only receives 40 percent of their preretirement income.

Pensions can also be problematic. Employer-sponsored plans are no longer common, and even if you are one of the few who receives a pension benefit, be aware that the amount you receive in retirement may not be more than 25 percent of your preretirement income.

That leaves personal savings. Faced with uncertainty and—at most—the limited payouts of Social Security and pension plans, the average American recognizes the need to find new ways to save some of their current income for retirement.

The good news? The government also realizes the importance of saving for retirement, so they have created several tax incentives to encourage Americans to save for retirement with pretax dollars.

Your Biggest Ally Is Time

Your financial advisor—any financial advisor—will tell you that the single most important component of saving for retirement is to start as soon as you can, regardless of how much you save. Compound interest is a powerful and wonderful thing, but it requires time to work. So the more time you have, the more your money will grow. It really is that simple.

If you have a 401(k) plan at work, or perhaps a traditional IRA, it can be extremely beneficial to begin saving as much as you can, as often as you can, even if it is only a few dollars a month. The old adage "every little bit helps" is never more accurate or true than when it pertains to saving. An additional bonus is that, in addition to saving money for retirement, you will also be reducing your taxable income in today's dollars by making these contributions. That means less money in taxes, and more for you when you retire. This is another powerful reason to begin saving today.

Follow the long-established golden rule of investing—do not put all your eggs in one basket.

Investing Is the Building Block of Retirement

Other than starting early, the biggest hurdle in saving for retirement—and certainly the source for most of your questions and worries—involves investments. Where should I invest? How do I know if my investments are right for me? Am I doing the right thing?

Fortunately, investing does not have to be complicated as long as you follow the long-established golden rule of investing—do not put all your eggs in one basket. You have probably heard that before, but it is worth hearing again. The fact is, as long as you spread your investments out across many companies and asset classes, you will minimize risk while increasing your chance of solid, dependable returns. And, as studies have shown, one of the most important things to remember is that working with a professional financial advisor will almost always help you achieve significantly better results than you would working alone. This has been tested and proven time and time again. Factor the enhanced results that come from working with a financial professional over a lifetime of savings and the difference is often life-changing.

Here is something to do: if your primary mode of saving is through a retirement plan with your employer, you will want to check to see if your plan offers any asset allocation investment funds. Asset allocation investment funds are funds that automatically invest your money in a way that is appropriate for your age or your investment objectives. If you do your own investment planning and are not comfortable making any drastic changes, you should ask a professional financial advisor to take a look at your plan to ensure you are doing what is best for you and your circumstances. Find an advisor with whom you feel comfortable. Interview him or her to be sure this person is someone with whom you want to work. It is important to feel confident that working with your financial planner will help you make the most of your current investments and enhance your planning—and your opportunity—to reach your retirement goals.

Bottom line, the best thing you can do to invest in your financial future can be summed up in two simple words: start today.

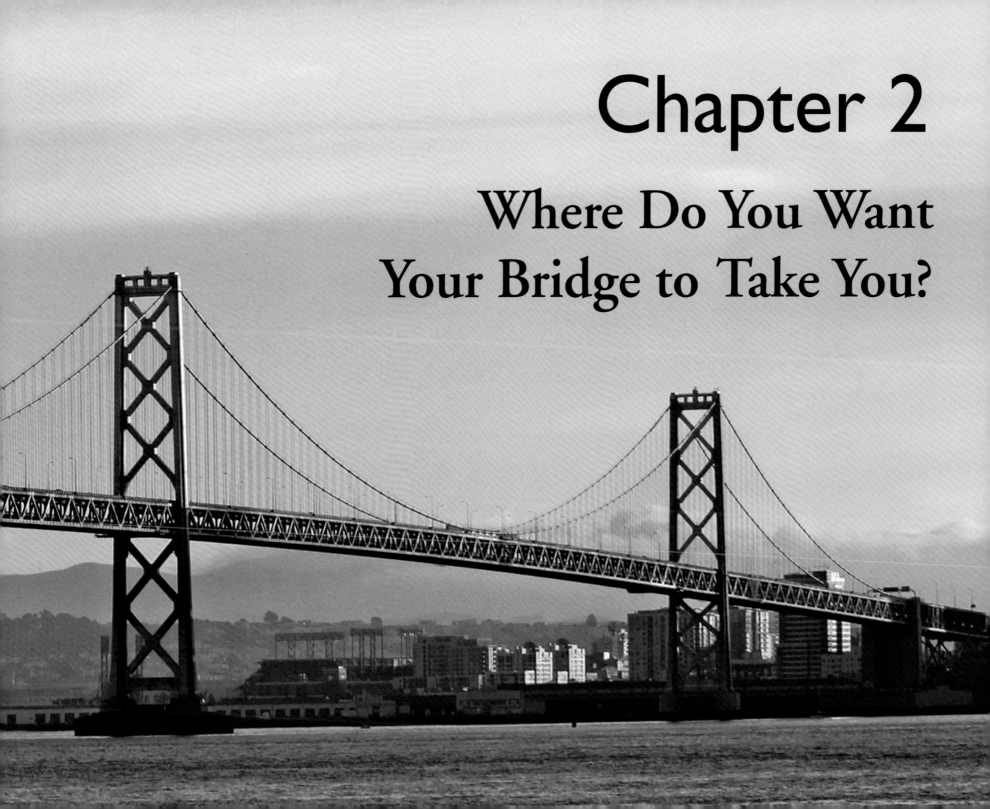

Chapter 2

Where Do You Want Your Bridge to Take You?

An organized retirement plan will give you confidence.

There is an old saying that goes like this: If you do not know where you are going, any road will take you there. Do you know which path you need to take? Do you need to provide for a college education? Retirement? Buying that house in the islands? Or do you simply want to have enough that you do not have to worry about having enough?

What Will Retirement Be Like for You?

What will it be like for you? Will you retire to a life of travel? Will you have the lifestyle you have always dreamed of or simply retreat to a rocking chair? Will you have to supplement your savings, or will you be able to focus on leisure activities and hobbies? Will your time be your own? An organized, comprehensive retirement plan can make the

the high seas. Hiking scenic mountains and canyons. Traveling around the country in an RV. Maybe you see yourself globe-trotting. Spending quality time with loved ones. Pursuing the hobbies and interests you never had time for during your busy income-earning years. Maybe you would like to live in an "active adult" community, living in a comfortable home with a low-maintenance yard, surrounded by new friends and acquaintances, with a golf course and other recreational amenities close at hand. All of these are specific goals, and they require a specific plan.

Life after Work: Redefining Retirement

Today, the concept of retirement has been redefined and does not mean what it used to. In fact, most people do not really "retire" anymore. The idea of simply fading away to life in a rocking chair is not part of the average person's vision of post-employment years. More accurately, most of us have come to realize that we need a way to segue from our working life to our life after work. For everyone contemplating eventual retirement, this is really the plan we need. And, like most types of planning that we do throughout life, it is never too early to start.

Regardless of your individual goals for "life after work," one thing is certain: the ideal plan allows you to enter this phase without financial worry, prepared to handle your living expenses and any emergencies that may arise, and perhaps still have something to leave for your heirs. Once

If you don't know where you're going, any road will take you there.

you reach retirement, you will want to enjoy your new life. A solid plan will help ensure that happens.

Enjoy is the key word here. Unfortunately, if you are like many people, you have probably given some thought to planning for your basic survival needs and maybe even your estate, but you have not made enjoyment of your senior years a major priority. This is where planning comes in.

Stop for a moment and really envision the retirement lifestyle you want. Let us consider some different scenarios:

A very basic retirement:

- You are comfortable in a small house with low utility bills.
- You plan on having no mortgage.
- You live, or plan to live, in a community with low taxes.
- You enjoy preparing and even growing your own food.
- Restaurant meals are not a necessity for you.
- You are happy driving older cars.
- You take occasional vacations by car, and you stay in modest hotels.
- You only shop for clothes when needed.
- You pay no club or membership dues.
- You will have no debt of any kind, including no car loans or leases.
- You are willing to work part-time.
- You need approximately $2,000 per month.
- You need $150,000–$500,000 in retirement funds, plus social security.

An average retirement:

- You enjoy a typical middle-class lifestyle and you want to keep it.
- The house you own now is adequate.
- Your house needs no major work and will be paid off by retirement.
- A dinner out and a movie is all the entertainment you desire.
- You will take periodic vacations, taking advantage of off-season rates.
- You do not feel the need to shop frequently.
- You like simple hobbies such as gardening, fishing, and reading.
- You have no credit card or automotive debt.
- You will work part-time if taxes or health care costs require it.
- You will need $2,000–$8,000 per month.
- You will need $500,000–$2 million in retirement funds.

A very comfortable retirement:

- You want to retire in a resort, beach, or golf development, or you want to retire in a big city and enjoy cosmopolitan amenities.
- You plan to join a gym or country club.
- You will probably own your home or condo.
- High taxes and association fees will be assessed annually.
- You plan to maintain nice furniture and new appliances.
- You enjoy restaurant meals two or three times a week.
- You enjoy new restaurants.
- You hope to take at least one great vacation in season each year.
- You want to maintain a closet full of nice clothes to wear frequently.

Fading away to life in a rocking chair is not part of the average person's vision of post-employment years.

- Social activities are important, and you plan to entertain often.
- You will need $8,000–$25,000 per month.
- You will need $2 million–$10 million in retirement funds.

A lavish retirement:

- You want to own, or already own, a large home in a very exclusive area.
- Utility bills on your home will total $1,000 or more a month.
- You own, or plan to own, more than one home.
- You plan to eat lunch and dinner mostly in restaurants and/or clubs.
- You plan to continue buying a new car every few years.
- You will belong to several clubs.
- You will have season tickets to sports and cultural events.
- You plan on taking luxury vacations and staying in four-star hotels.
- You normally spend $1,000 or more a month on discretionary items.
- When you read magazines, you pick out things to buy in the ads.
- You will need $50,000–$100,000 per month.
- You will need at least approximately $10 million in retirement funds.

So there you have it. It may not be as easy as simply picking the lifestyle you want, but you have to start setting parameters at some point. If you are unsure of the retirement lifestyle that is realistic or achievable for you, or if you know the lifestyle you desire but have no real idea of how to get there, a trained, tenured wealth advisor can help you build a blueprint to make it achievable.

Build a blueprint to make it achievable.

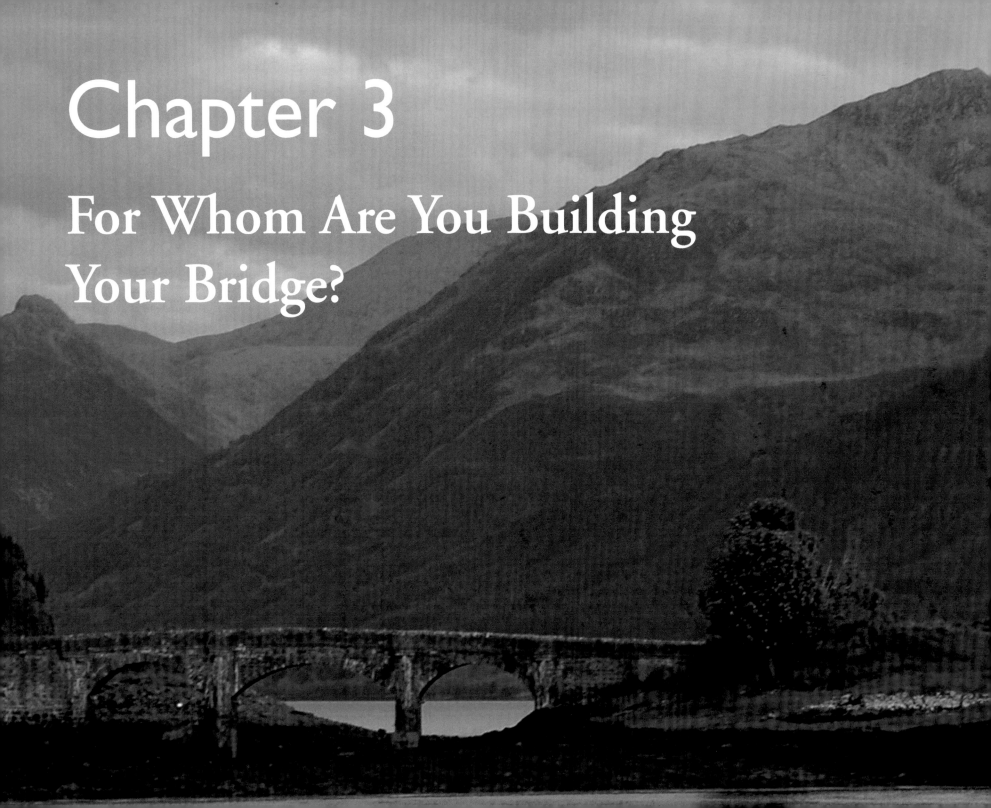

Chapter 3

For Whom Are You Building Your Bridge?

Having someone depend on you
is all the incentive you need.

For most of us, the bridge we build is designed to carry those who depend on us now or those who will follow us later. Make sure your bridge is wide enough to accommodate all of the important people in your life.

Having someone depend on you is all the incentive you need to formulate a successful plan.

If you have dependents counting on you, it is important to start securing your family's future as soon as possible by making sensible financial decisions.

Of course, when it comes to providing for your family's long-term financial wealth, any prudent long-term investment will help. In addition to those things you might typically think of, there are several other things you might not initially consider that will go a long way toward helping you achieve long-term financial stability.

Ten Basic Steps

1. Earn What You Are Worth and Spend Less Than You Earn

That sounds almost too simple, but many people struggle with this first basic rule. Make sure you know what your skills are worth in the marketplace, and do all you can do to ensure you are paid what you are worth. Being underpaid even a thousand dollars a year can have a significant cumulative effect over the course of your working life.

Of course, no matter how much or how little you are paid, you will never get ahead if you spend more than you earn. Oftentimes it is easier to spend less than it is to earn more, and a little cost-cutting effort in a number of areas can result in big savings. It does not always have to involve making big sacrifices.

2. Stick to a Budget

Budgeting is perhaps the single most important thing you can do. How can you know how much you spend or where your money is going if you do not budget? And how can you set saving goals if you do not know where your money is going? Unfortunately, most people overlook this most basic and valuable tool, or think they can always budget "later." Remember, you need a budget regardless of the salary you earn or how young—or not so young—you are.

Saving does not always have to involve making big sacrifices.

3. Pay Off Credit Card Debt

Credit card debt is the number one obstacle to getting ahead financially. Those small plastic cards are often too easy to use, and it is easy to forget that we are dealing with real money when we use them. Despite intentions to pay the balance off quickly, the reality is that people often do not and they end up paying far more for things than if they simply used cash.

4. Contribute to a Retirement Plan

If your employer has a 401(k) plan and you do not contribute to it, you are walking away from one of the best deals available to you. Ask your employer if the company offers a 401(k) plan or something similar and sign up today. If you are already contributing, try to increase your contribution. If your employer does not offer a retirement plan, consider an IRA. Either way, make sure you leverage your earnings by using these tools properly.

5. Have a Savings Plan

The single easiest way to have a savings plan is something you have probably heard before. Pay yourself first. Most people think of savings as "what is left over" after paying for everything else. Unfortunately, if you wait until you have met all your other financial obligations to save, chances are you will never have a healthy savings account or investments.

The single easiest way to have a savings plan: pay yourself first.

23

A quick fix for this is to set aside a minimum of 5 percent to 10 percent of your salary for saving before you start paying bills. Better yet, have money automatically deducted from your paycheck and deposited into a separate account. It is easiest to do this when you simply look at this percentage as a debt you owe that you must pay monthly. If you think about it clearly and realistically, the fact is that you do owe it to yourself and your family! Taking this one simple step can be your start toward the retirement you want.

6. Invest

If you are contributing to a retirement plan and a savings account and you can still manage to put some money into other investments, you should. At the very least, consider some basic items:

Mutual Funds: If you have the right funds, mutual funds can offer a unique and favorable combination of low cost, flexibility, and tax efficiency.

Children's Savings Accounts: It goes without saying that it is important to plan for your child's future. It is equally important that you teach your child the value of saving. One of the best ways to do this is to open a children's savings account and teach your child to deposit money in it every month.

Stocks and Bonds: Owning stocks and bonds outright can provide good solid returns, but this often comes with an increased short-term risk.

7. Maximize Your Employment Benefits

Make sure you really know what benefits are offered by your employer. This is another point in the planning cycle where a trained professional can provide beneficial insight. Take the time to really understand how employment benefits like a 401(k) plan, profit sharing, flexible spending accounts, medical and dental insurance, and others can be valuable financial resources for you. Making sure you are maximizing your benefits by taking advantage of these can save you money by reducing taxes or out-of-pocket expenses.

Making sure you are maximizing your benefits can save you money.

8. Review Your Insurance

Insurance is important, especially if you have dependents. Term life insurance can do an adequate job of covering risk and is the least expensive insurance you can buy to protect your loved ones. No other area is more confusing to consumers. Too many people pay too much for life and disability insurance while others add insurance they may not need, such as buying life insurance when you have no dependents. It is important that you have enough insurance to protect your dependents and your income in the case of death or disability. Long-term care (LTC) planning should also be included in this review. LTC planning is, in my experience, the most overlooked predeath planning out there. A review of all your insurance coverage and needs can provide a valuable service to you and your family by preventing you from over- or under-insuring yourself.

9. Update Your Will

Most Americans do not have a will. In almost every circumstance, no matter how little or how much you own, you need a will if you have dependents. Think of it as protecting your loved ones. Durable powers of attorney for medical, financial, and HIPAA information disclosure as well as Directives to Physicians are very important. If you do not have a will, contact a qualified attorney and take care of that responsibility.

10. Keep Good Records

If you do not keep good records, you are not likely to benefit from all of your allowable income tax deductions and credits. Set up a system now and use it all year. It is much easier than scrambling to find everything at tax time, only to miss items that might have saved you money. Even a small amount saved here once each year can have significant long-term benefits for you and your family. An updated financial plan with current copies of your investment reports, will and collateral documents, insurance policies, and financial and retirement plans should be kept in an accessible spot for your heirs. This information should be updated on an annual basis at the very least.

There you have it—a rudimentary plan consisting of ten easy steps that will help you maximize your financial wealth.

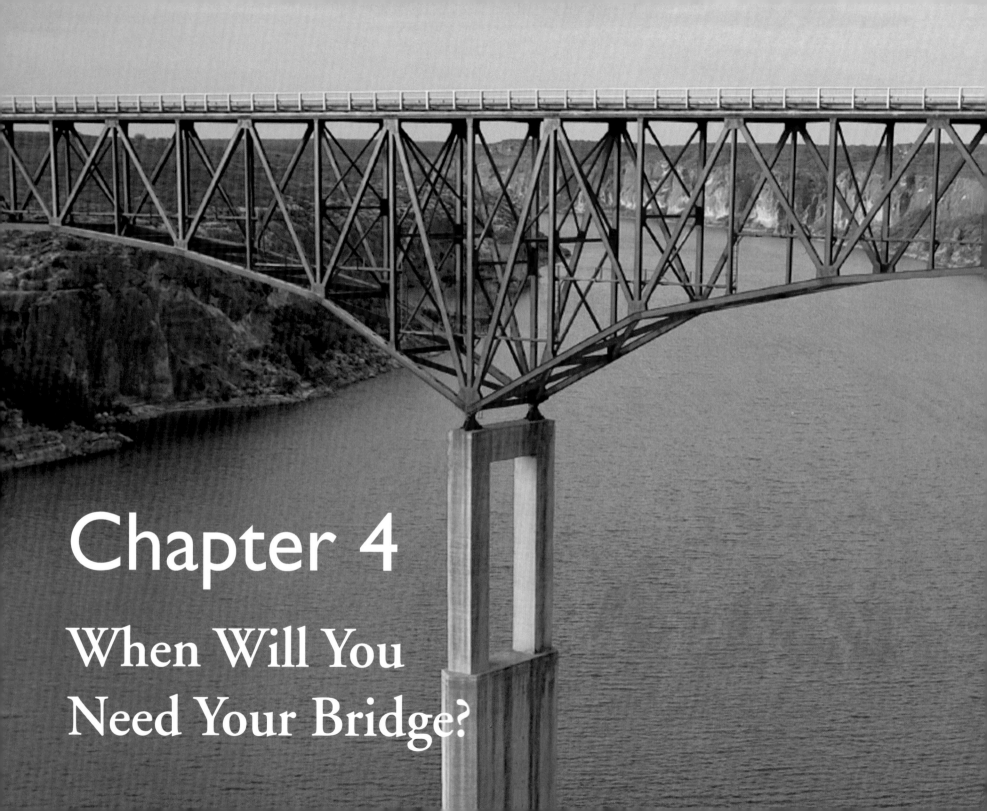

Chapter 4

When Will You Need Your Bridge?

How do you want to spend
the rest of your life?

When should you retire? What will you need to be able to retire?
What kind of investing will you still want to do? How do you want to
spend the rest of your life? Do you want to move to a sunnier place with
a warmer climate? Downsize? Upsize? Try a new hobby? Give money to
a charity? When will all of this take place?

When Should You Retire?

The answer to the question "when should I retire?" can vary
significantly from individual to individual depending on any number of
factors: how much you like your job, how long you expect to live, what
you actually want to do with the rest of your life and—of course—the
size of your savings. It seems basic, but assuring yourself that there is
a reasonable chance you will not outlive your retirement assets is the
first step.

Workers who stay on the job can significantly increase their retirement income.

Consider these facts: the traditional retirement age in this country is sixty-five. But workers who stay on the job until sixty-seven and increase their 401(k) contribution rate by 2 percent (for example, from 6 percent of salary to 8 percent) can significantly increase their retirement income.

For workers who will not receive a pension or company-provided retiree medical benefits, working longer can be a particularly beneficial strategy.

Should You Retire?

Perhaps an even better question is whether you should retire at all. This is a life-altering decision on many levels and therefore an important one. Here are a few tips to make your decision a little easier:

- What is your age? If you are fifty-five to sixty-five, retirement may or may not seem attractive to you. Consider your age and remember that we only have so many years. What would you still like to accomplish with those remaining years? Do you want to travel? Do you have any goals you would fulfill if it were not for work? If there are, then maybe you should factor in these goals and lay out a timetable for your retirement and activities afterwards.

- How is your health? Are you in good health, or is your health making it more difficult to work? Or worse—is your work contributing to a decline in your health? Is your health making work more uncomfortable for you as time passes by? You may

want to check with a doctor for a total health evaluation before deciding to continue with work.

- Does your family affect your decision? Some people will want to spend more time with their families as they age. For others, their family members may want them to retire for any number of reasons. You may want to consider your family's wishes regarding your decision to retire.

- How are your finances? Will you be financially capable of sustaining your lifestyle long after retirement? If your retirement savings cannot keep up with your desired spending lifestyle after retirement, you may want to work and save for a little longer. A complete financial plan should include these calculations and answer these questions.

- Will you retire late? An important thing to consider is the fact that some retirement plans become more attractive if you retire later. In some cases, your retirement income can be significantly affected for the better by working for just a few additional years.

Also, you have to consider whether you have saved enough to handle unexpected items, such as medical emergencies and the rising cost of living. If you can, you may indeed want to retire early.

Finally, remember that many people who retire—especially those who retire early—often find out that life without a real occupation on

which to focus can sometimes be very boring. For this reason many people, even though they do not need to financially, often work part-time as a consultant or fill in for those on vacation. If you like being busy, you may want to spend some time before you retire thinking about what you will do to keep busy.

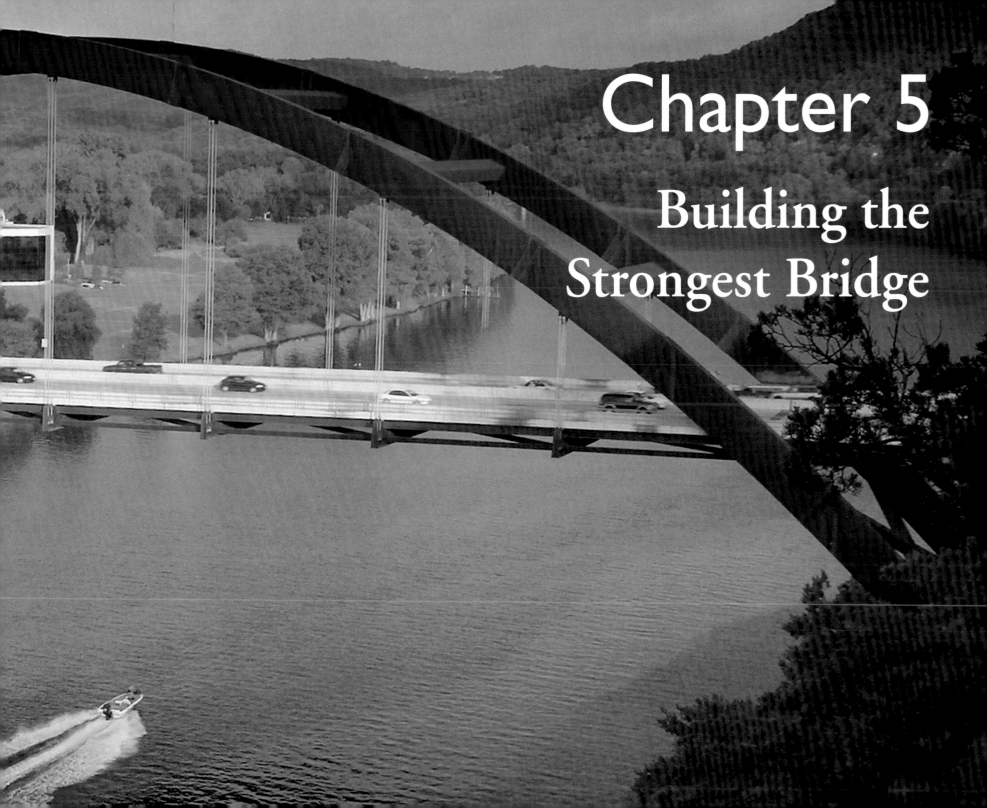

Chapter 5
Building the
Strongest Bridge

How long do you expect to live? We all face the prospect of unanticipated tragedies but we must be optimistic for retirement planning. If you are a sixty-five-year-old couple, odds are that one of you will live into your nineties. Whatever your age, your plan should fund your lifespan before your lifestyle. Building a strong bridge to longevity is essential.

Construction Step One:
Plan for a Long Life

Ronald Manheimer, executive director of the North Carolina Center for Creative Retirement at the University of North Carolina at Asheville, says about one-third of Americans are really working on a post-retirement action plan, but one-third are "completely clueless." To help people through this phase of their lives, Manheimer has started a "life transition program for boomers" to help them figure out what they want to do in retirement. You can check out his program at www.unca.edu/ncccr/.

Basic bridge-building for most people should begin when they become fully responsible for their care and income. You should

1. Control debt.
2. Establish and maintain an emergency savings plan.
3. Make regular contributions to a retirement savings plan, no matter how small the contribution, and discipline yourself to put a portion of every income increase into savings.
4. Develop and follow a diet and exercise plan for good health.
5. As soon as you have someone dependent on you for care, work with a qualified estate planning attorney to create the appropriate will and collateral documents for your current stage of life.

As you move toward your major earning years (30–50 for most people), you should

1. Pay down your debt and stay on track to be debt free by retirement.
2. Continue your retirement contributions and begin gradually changing your investment strategy to fit your approaching life transition.
3. Update your estate planning documents at least every ten years— or when you have a major change in your life such as marriage, divorce, inheritance, or the birth of a child.

Bridge-building should begin when you become responsible for your care and income.

Three to five years prior to leaving full-time employment or business ownership and beginning to let your investments support you, you should

1. Reallocate your investments to suit your new risk profile—as you get closer to retirement, you will have less time to make up any losses.

2. Look closely at your budget and change your lifestyle so that your savings will support you throughout your remaining lifespan.

3. Work to close the gap between retirement savings and the amount of money needed for a comfortable retirement.

4. Downsize your home if necessary.

5. Review your entire plan with a qualified financial planner.

6. Remember, lifespan needs to be funded before lifestyle.

Construction Step Two:
Marshal Your Forces in Retirement

Now you are on your way to a new lifestyle. Your plans are in place, your safety fund and savings are reallocated and matched to your current risk tolerance, and all your documents are updated. During this period just prior to retirement, you need to give consideration to your state of mind. Will you have enough to keep you busy in this new lifestyle? Is charitable work or perhaps travel on the horizon?

Finally, you will need to give consideration to your long-term care (LTC) needs. Eventually we still have to face LTC issues and the end stage of our lives. This is the final stage of financial planning for our lives,

> Will you have enough to keep you busy in this new lifestyle?

and it is one of the most critical. Proper estate planning documents, end-of-life plans, and provisions to fund the costs of caregivers are critical. Peace of mind for these final years comes from a strong financial bridge that supports life-span planning. Without the experience of a tenured financial planner and estate planner, these can be easily overlooked and underestimated. A great place to start is with the book, *There's No Place Like (A Nursing) Home* by Karen Shoff.

Construction Step Three:
Independence Day

One day you work; the next day you don't. Some people are prepared and enjoy their new freedom; others crash and burn. It is very important that you take time to consider what you will do when you enter this next phase of your life before you take the plunge. Hobbies, social groups, travel, and charitable work are just a few of the things that could fill your time. Start by asking yourself a question Dan Sullivan uses in *The Strategic Coach*. He calls it the "R-Factor Question," and it goes like this:

The R-Factor Question® *

"If we were meeting here three years from today—and you were to look back over those three years to today—what has to have happened during that period, both personally and professionally, for you to feel happy about your progress?"

Make a checklist of things you want to

- See—places, people, or events.
- Learn—cooking, dancing, sailing, art history, or painting.
- Speak—languages help you enjoy travel and appreciate ethnic cultures.
- Practice—exercise routines, daily walks, or weekly book club meetings.
- Contribute to charities—serving meals, rescuing animals, or tutoring children.
- That's just the beginning. Start your own list and fill it with your dreams. Then make them reality.

Construction Step Four:
Seeing Your Bridge and Crossing It

Fortunately, most people who retire are relatively young and in good health. Most have goals and set out eagerly to pursue them. According to research by financial services conglomerate HSBC, 73 percent of Americans say travel is the number one activity they want to pursue when they retire. There is no slowing down and resting for these folks during the first couple of years of retirement. They do not share the same vision of retirement their parents had.

After this initial burst of energy, people begin to fit into a pattern of actions that can lead to concern and unhappiness over their finances. This is a critical point in retirement. Planning needs to be done pre-

With proper planning, this period of your life can be a rich and rewarding time.

retirement to avoid this period of decline in enjoyment and enthusiasm. The Center for Retirement Research at Boston College found that 43 percent of working households in 2004 were at risk of having too little income to fund retirement, which was up from 31 percent in 1983—a jarring increase.

In defense of many retirees, when they hit this slick spot, they react in a positive fashion. Not everyone gets "depressed." They go out and reinvent themselves, slow down, and seek a simpler but even more abundant life. If you have planned properly, you do not have to be part of the crowd that is struggling, unhappy, and dissatisfied.

With proper planning, this period of your life can be a rich and rewarding time when you can provide invaluable guidance to future generations by your actions and advice. Do not waste the opportunity by leaving your future to chance.

Chapter 6

The Foundation of Your Bridge Is the Key

It is never too early to begin construction.

Like any structure on which you depend, the bridge to your financial future will only be as strong as its foundation.

Planning for your future requires you to be able to answer three basic questions:

- Where are you today?
- Where do you want to be?
- How can you reach your destination?

Closing the gap between where you are and where you wish to be is only made possible by a strong, safe bridge. It is never too early to begin construction.

Preparing the Foundation

Preparing the foundation for the bridge to your financial future involves organization and homework. It is the kind of task that often

gets put on an "I'll do it whenever I get around to it" list, which usually gets lost and, inevitably, forgotten.

There is an easy way to avoid this scenario. Hire an advocate and advisor who can guide you through this process and help you fit it into your busy schedule. An experienced advisor can skillfully lead you through this process by reviewing your financial history, thoroughly discussing your needs and goals with you, and recommending financial plans tailored specifically to you and your long-term goals. Paying attention to personal detail will always make a huge difference in the success of your planning.

Here are some of the areas you will address when your financial advisor sets out to help you build the foundation for your life's journey:

Determine your short-term and long-term financial objectives:

This is important, because you need to have a destination in mind before you can begin the journey.

Know your net worth (assets versus liabilities):

Do you know yours?

Evaluate your credit worthiness:

Get copies of your credit report. Errors on these reports are common, so it is important to study them carefully for accuracy.

Do you know your net worth?

Create a realistic budget:

This is critical. Track your spending and make saving a top priority in your life, regardless of how much you can commit to saving right now.

Determine your family's future education needs:

How many children? Private or public schools? Undergraduate, graduate, or both? All of these are issues that need to be thought through at some point.

Assess your insurance needs, including every type of insurance you may or may not need: disability, long-term care, property/casualty, health, and life.

Make Sure You Cover Your Bases

From time to time, most people undergo some sort of financial emergency. For that reason, everyone needs a financial safety net to take care of basic needs and potential emergencies during those times of financial stress. The more numerous your responsibilities, the larger your safety net needs to be. From there, more specific goals can be identified and plans implemented for achieving them.

Creating such a long-term plan can be an intimidating, perhaps overwhelming project to tackle alone. A professional financial advisor can help break it into all the steps needed to help you fulfill your needs and your dreams.

Creating such a long-term plan can be an intimidating, perhaps overwhelming project to tackle alone.

Bottom line: the right financial advisor should be able to help you gain a concrete knowledge of what it takes to retire, how to get there, and how to keep your retirement securely funded. Moving toward retirement is a journey, and one of the best ways to enjoy it is to know that you have a sound and safe financial plan in place that will care for you and your family when the time comes.

Ask yourself some basic questions to make sure your portfolio does not contain unnecessary risk.

Most investors worry about risk. Without professional advice, though, it can be very difficult to determine if your portfolio is exposed to unnecessary risk and if so, how to remove it?

Let us consider a few basic questions: Are you confident that you know your true return on investment (ROI) over the last year or the last five years? How does that return compare to the performance of an index such as the S&P 500 Index? Does it meet your life goal for return?

Or ask yourself this: if any of the following were to occur, would your portfolio be protected from significant loss?

- Terrorist attack
- Depression
- Recession
- Hyper inflation
- Stagflation (rising costs and interest rates with a weakening economy)
- Significant devaluation in the dollar

Everyone needs a financial safety net to take care of basic needs and potential emergencies during times of financial stress.

What happens if something happens to you?

Here is an even bigger and more important question: do you really know what happens if something happens to you? Write these questions down and write your answer beside them. If you do not know the answer, you may be at risk.

If something were to happen to you, do your spouse and/or family members understand your entire financial picture well enough to carry on without you? People are living longer and health care costs are soaring, which means that planning ahead is more important now than ever.

Use the following list of questions to make sure that you are on track for a healthy, wealthy retirement with a plan that has minimized risk.

- Does your current portfolio contain "off the shelf" generic investments with hidden fees and potential conflicts of interest?

- Have you defined in writing what financial freedom means to you?

- Have you written down your financial goals and the necessary objectives to achieve them?

- Are you exposed to paying significantly more taxes than necessary? Whatever your answer is, how do you know for sure?

- How long has it been since you updated your estate plan? Frequent changes affect estate and tax planning. Has your plan been reviewed and updated by a professional within the past twelve months?

Chapter 7
Paying for Your Bridge

The simple arithmetic of managing your financial future is defined in many ways. Some say it is as simple as spending less and saving more. Here are some basic financial parameters you need to consider, regardless of your age or how late you started planning for your financial future.

Are You Part of the 43 Percent?

Recent research suggests that most people do not know how much they need to save for retirement. In fact, research by the Employee Benefit Research Institute's 2007 Retirement Confidence Study found that only 43 percent of workers have actually tried to calculate how much they need to save for a secure retirement. Although everyone understands the importance of saving for retirement, less than half of us have ever bothered to figure out what we need.

It Does Not Have to Be Complicated

If you have a garden, you know that you have to plant bulbs in the fall if you expect to have a rich color display in the spring. Financial planning works the same way. Taking small steps now to prepare for success in the future is the basic premise of retirement planning. Again, though, not everyone prepares. A good and, unfortunately, common example is the 401(k) many people have at work. With the power of compounding, putting even a minimal amount of money in your 401(k) over time is like planting seeds that will eventually grow into magnificent trees. However, if you do not plant the seeds, the tree will never grow.

How to Jump-Start Your Retirement Saving:
Power of Compounding

By now you should understand that it is good to start as soon as possible by signing up with your employer's 401(k) plan. Remember—even small contributions can make a big difference. If a husband and wife each save $10 a day starting at age fifty-two and invest it in mutual funds that give them an average rate of return of 8 percent (not unreasonable if they diversify their portfolio and invest for the long term), by age seventy they will have $294,449 in savings. If their employers match 50 percent of their contributions, their nest egg could grow to $441,673 during that time.

However, if you do
not plant the seeds, the tree
will never grow.

Saving Future Income

Here is a good way to think about it: when you put money into a 401(k), you are making sure that some of the salary you are earning today will be available when you need it after you retire. Instead of that money coming home in your paycheck this week, it goes directly into your retirement account. In other words, you are just postponing when you will receive that portion of your salary.

Maximize Tax Benefits

Contributing to a savings plan like a 401(k) also saves on taxes. For example, assume that you deposit $100 into your account. Once you do that, the full $100 goes to work for you. If you do not contribute the money and keep it as "take-home pay," and if you are, for instance, in the 20 percent tax bracket, you would only see $80 of it after taxes. That is quite a benefit you are giving up by not contributing, so why would you not do it?

What about your employer match? Do not forget to take advantage of your employer's matching contribution. Not doing so means that you are, essentially, declining free money. Do you really want to turn your back on free money? Remember, it is there for the taking.

As a professional financial advisor, I have too often seen people build a financial plan and then put it on the shelf to collect dust, assuming that their job is done. A comprehensive review of your financial plan once a year is critical to keeping it current.

Do you really want to turn your back on free money?

Get a financial checkup
once each year, just as you should
physically. Retirement goals can,
and do, change.

Think of It Logically

Building a long-term plan for retirement is one of the most important financial challenges you will face in your lifetime. Once you have done that, does it not make sense to review and monitor it often to make sure it remains a viable plan?

Get a financial checkup once each year, just as you should physically. Retirement goals can and do change. Once a year, you owe it to yourself to ask yourself the following:

- Do the goals I originally set still apply?
- Do I still plan to retire at the age I first envisioned?
- Has an illness or other life event changed my retirement goals?
- Are my investments growing in a manner to finance my retirement goals?

It is important to periodically reevaluate your goals and possibly set new ones; change elsewhere in our lives tends to be constant. An annual financial review will make sure your planning keeps up with your life.

Have your personal finances changed? Is your income more or less than when you originally set up your retirement plan? Do you have additional income to invest from a second job or your spouse's job? Have you had a bankruptcy or made major purchases in the past few years that might affect your retirement plan? Do you have children in college that might dip into your retirement funds? Have you had to withdraw some of your retirement investments for personal use? Your circumstances at any given time will dictate what you can put back for your retirement.

Have your spending habits changed? Has your spending changed significantly since you last reviewed your retirement plan? Before you say no, consider some of the many innocuous ways that spending changes in our lifetime:

- You get married.
- You get divorced.
- You have a child.
- You change jobs.
- You buy a home.
- You make a large purchase.
- You start saving.
- You stop saving.

Look at your budget and see if there are ways you can free up some extra money to put aside for your retirement. If you see you are putting too much aside, you might use the extra for a much-needed vacation.

Does your portfolio fit you and your age? Carefully scrutinizing how your portfolio is balanced at least once each year will help you get the most out of your investments. Why does your age matter? Well, your age and how close you are to retirement will dictate whether your portfolio will consist of investments for growth, income, or a combination of both. If you have not done so in a while, now is a good time to look

Does your portfolio fit you and your age?

at the companies you have invested in to be sure they are performing satisfactorily. If you are not sure, ask a competent financial advisor.

Do you know where you stand with Social Security? If you have not already done so, you should get a statement of earnings from the Social Security Administration (SSA) so that you understand clearly what you can expect to earn when you retire. Another reason to review this statement is to make sure there are no mistakes in your account. The form can be ordered online from the SSA. Look over the figures on the statement and if you have questions or find a mistake, call the SSA immediately.

Where will your health and life insurance come from? If you are working, chances are you have both health and life insurance provided through your employer—will these still be available when you retire? Some companies offer both to retirees, but some do not. What will happen if you leave employment before retirement age? Have you made provisions for health and life insurance coverage or at least discussed these with your financial advisor?

Is your employer retirement plan out-of-sight and out-of-mind? Does your company offer a pension plan? If so, do you know what type of plan it is? Does your company offer matching funds? Are you contributing all you can to the plan? Can you choose the investments or are they chosen for you? Do you know how well they are doing? Are you vested? How long does it take to be vested? What happens to

Is your pension plan out-of-sight and out-of-mind?

> The closer you get to retirement age, the more often you will want to review your plan.

your retirement plan if you leave the company? How much is your plan worth right now and how much can you expect it to grow between now and next year?

Do you have an IRA? If you have an IRA, would it be more beneficial to roll it over into a Roth IRA? Is your IRA earning you the best possible return? When can you roll it over to another fund?

Like any other plan, your retirement plan should be reviewed periodically to be sure it is performing in the way you need. The closer you get to retirement age, the more often you will want to review your plan. And, as always, discuss it with your financial planner if at all possible.

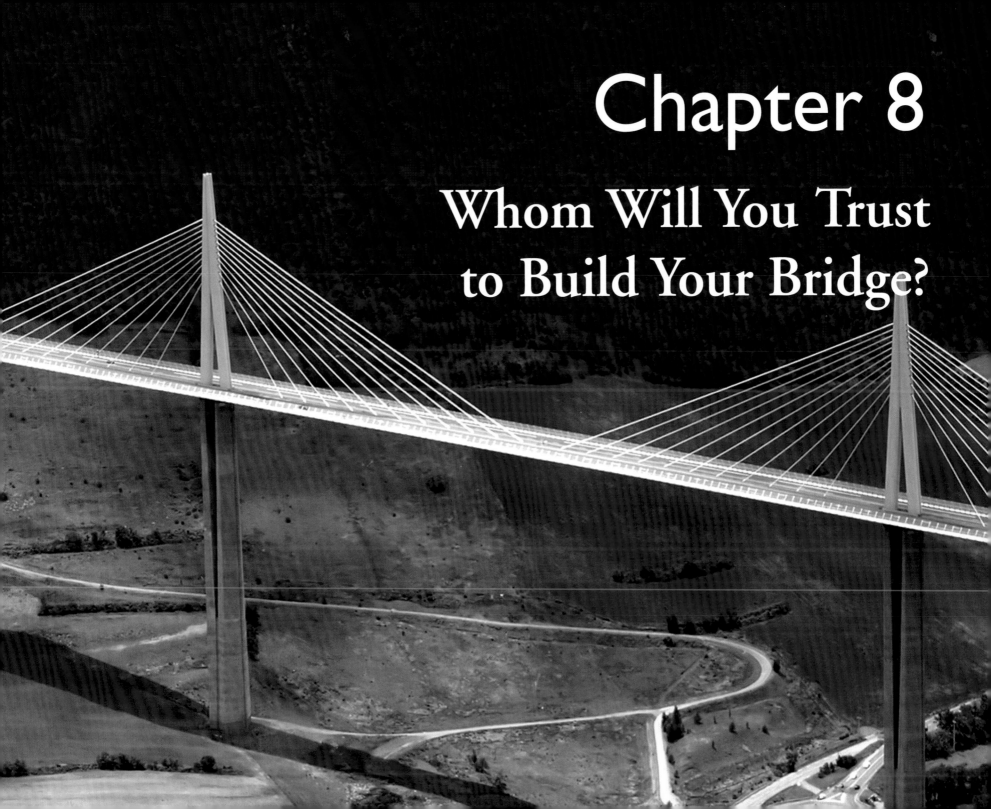

Chapter 8

Whom Will You Trust to Build Your Bridge?

Know the kind of retirement you
want, and create a plan to reach it.

The architect of your bridge will determine the long-term value of
your bridge to you. Choosing the right financial advisor is one of the
most important financial decisions you will make in your life. As with
the selection of all professionals, choose an advisor who can demonstrate
training, tenure, and a track record.

Creating the Plan

Once you know the kind of retirement you want, it is time to create
the plan that will help you reach it. Remember, just because you may be
able to buy the materials to build the bridge yourself, it is not necessarily
a good idea to design and build it alone. You need an architect to ensure
it is built to the highest standards. In this case, of course, the architect is
a financial advisor.

A good advisor should be your sounding board.

Historically, investors who have worked with a financial advisor have consistently—and significantly—outperformed do-it-yourself investors. This should come as no surprise to anyone. For instance, in the United States alone there are more than ten thousand different mutual funds to choose from. Throw in the assortment of international funds, plus the natural fluctuations in national and international economic conditions, and making the best choice among thousands becomes even more difficult without the guidance of an experienced professional. The biggest issue, of course, is that professional investment advisors have access to specialized research, comprehensive performance data, and other tools to assist in helping you achieve your financial goals to which the average person simply does not have access.

A good financial advisor will help you with much more than simply choosing appropriate investments for your money. He or she will help you identify your long-term goals and help define appropriate strategies to achieve these. Examples include: retirement planning, education savings for your dependents, early retirement, or saving to purchase a vacation home.

A good advisor should be your sounding board for major decisions, such as buying a house, and be available to answer your financial questions whenever they come up. Even more importantly, your advisor should be someone that you trust and who takes the time to understand your particular financial situation thoroughly. Finally, a good advisor will not only explain the importance of diversifying your investments but will also help you come up with an investment plan that takes your own goals and level of risk tolerance into account. He or she will be there to answer your questions, reassure you, and keep you focused on your long-term plan. This can be especially valuable when the market turns sour and your investments do not provide the results you were expecting.

One of the best ways to find a good financial advisor is to ask for referrals from friends, family members, or a trusted lawyer or accountant. It is important to find an advisor who you believe has your interests at heart, and who does not mind spending time with you.

Once you have found a potential advisor, ask him or her for the name of clients he or she has worked with and—here is the important part— phone these people to gauge their level of satisfaction with the advisor. Satisfied clients are a good financial advisor's best report card. If an advisor cannot or will not give you current clients with whom to speak, consider that a warning sign.

In addition, stay away from advisors who are pushing products that pay commissions. Advisors who categorically recommend that you avoid putting your money into debt repayment or real estate purchases are probably also hoping to sell you a commissioned product. If an advisor is selling legal services and wants to do your income tax return themselves, you should rightfully wonder about this person's particular area of expertise.

Satisfied clients are a good financial advisor's best marketing tools.

Finally, if an advisor is trying to unnecessarily scare you or make you dependent on him or her by exaggerating the complexity of your financial situation, you should run away as fast as you can. Other than these caveats, go with your gut as you would in choosing any other professional, such as a doctor or lawyer.

Questions to Ask a Potential Financial Advisor

Something you will definitely want to know is who pays your advisor and for whom he or she works. In reality, some investment advisors have a conflict of interest when dealing with clients. For instance, do you know how your advisor is compensated and whether or not it compromises his or her ability to put your interests first? Before seriously considering an investment advisor, consider examining some key preliminary information:

Comprehensive services provided:

- Goal setting?
- Cash management?
- Cash budgeting?
- Tax planning?
- Investment review?
- Investment planning?
- Estate planning?
- Insurance needs?
- Education funding?

In reality, some investment advisors have a conflict of interest when dealing with clients. Choose your advisor carefully.

- Retirement planning?
- Other services offered?

Type(s) of advice provided:

- Written analysis?
- Formal recommendations?
- Provide implementation?
- Provide ongoing advice?

Educational background:

- College degree in financial advising?
- Graduate degree?
- If not, primary area of study?

Certifications/credentials:

- Is he or she licensed?
- By whom?
- NAPFA-Registered Financial Advisor
- Masters degree in Financial Planning (MBA)
- Certified Financial Planner (CFP)
- Chartered Financial Consultant (ChFC)
- Certified Public Accountant (CPA)
- Personal Financial Specialist (PFS)
- Financial Planning Association (FPA)
- Other Certifications?

When choosing a financial advisor, go with tenure, training, and a track record.

Experience:

- Years as a financial advisor?
- Have you spoken with existing clients of this advisor?

Compensation:

- Affiliated with an insurance company?
- Affiliated with a bank or financial institution?
- Any organization for which they sell products?
- How, specifically, are they paid?
  - Fee only
  - Commissions
  - Fee based (fee and commissions)
  - Fee offset

Regulatory:

- Any complaints filed against them?
- More importantly, any disciplinary actions?
- Is he/she a registered investment advisor?
- Have they signed a Fiduciary Oath?

Connection:

- Do you like the advisor?
- Is this someone with whom you would like to work?

A good financial advisor will help you with much more than simply choosing appropriate investments for your money.

The good news:
you have plenty of choices
when it comes to working with
financial professionals.

You do not have to ask all these questions, but you should certainly ask enough to reach a comfort level regarding what a potential advisor can do for you in helping you plan long-term goals. You should also feel comfortable regarding their ability to make the plan a reality. This is one of the most important decisions you will make in your life. Make sure you are comfortable with it for all the right reasons.

Which Professionals Will Help You Build Your Bridge?

Here is the good news: you have plenty of choices when it comes to working with financial professionals. However, before you begin choosing those professionals, it might be smart to think about all the help you need to reach your financial goals. Your answers to the following questions can point you in the right direction.

What Are the Financial Issues for Which You Need Help?

It is smart to consider precisely with what you would like a financial professional's help. For example:

- Work with you to identify your life goals?
- Develop and implement an investment plan?
- Provide ongoing advice?
- Purchase a long-term care policy?

- Assist with very specific concerns, such as choosing the most advantageous 529 college savings plan?
- Develop a retirement savings plan for your small business?

Once you decide exactly with what you need help, you can match your needs to the expertise and experience of a financial professional.

What Kind of Professionals Will You Need?

Financial Planners

Financial planners generally take a very broad view of your financial affairs and function as your personal chief investment officer. The most comprehensive of these financial planners will help you assess and manage every aspect of your financial life, including your savings, investments, insurance, taxes, retirement, and estate planning. The best financial planners work with you to identify your long-term financial goals, work diligently to help you develop a plan to meet those goals, and regularly review your progress with you in person. In many cases, these planners also manage your investment portfolio for you.

Investment Advisors

Investment advisors usually focus specifically on managing your investments. They also, of course, provide financial advice and some investment advisors are financial planners. The majority, though, are focused on providing you with sound investment advice, and are compensated on an annual basis by a percentage of the assets they manage for you.

Match your needs to the expertise and experience of a financial professional.

Stockbrokers

These professionals traditionally have served as intermediaries between buyers and sellers of stocks and bonds; typically they were compensated by commissions. However, today there are brokers who, while still living on commissions, also provide some financial planning advice.

Insurance Agents

A licensed insurance agent can help you with insurance needs from property and casualty insurance to life insurance and annuities. Also, he or she can help you sort out health insurance and long-term care options, as well as offer overall risk management strategies.

CPA/Accountants

A CPA is a professional licensed by a state to offer a variety of accounting services such as simple tax preparation, financial audits, business valuations, and succession planning for small businesses.

Estate Planning Attorneys

These lawyers focus on estate needs and perform valuable, needed service. For instance, they can draft your will, write durable powers of attorney and health care proxies, or work with your financial advisors to develop sophisticated wealth transfer strategies to ensure your estate passes to your heirs in the most tax efficient manner. In addition to creating trusts so your assets can pass to your beneficiaries, estate planning attorneys can also develop strategies that enable favorite charities to benefit from your generosity.

Work with someone you like.

How Will You Pay for Professional Services?

Financial professionals charge for their services in any number of ways, so it is important that you understand how yours gets paid before hiring them. Also make sure that it matches how you want to pay. Below are some of the ways many financial professionals are paid:

- A percentage of the value of the assets they manage for you
- An hourly fee for the time they spend working for you
- A fixed or retainer fee
- A commission on the products they place
- Some combination of the above

Each compensation method has its own unique potential benefits and/or possible drawbacks, depending on your specific needs, so make sure you understand whom you are paying, when you are paying them, for what services, under which circumstances, and how often.

The Process

Finally, it is important to work with someone you like. You will spend time with this person on a regular basis, so it is important that this be someone you do not mind being around. And while a financial professional may have all the right qualifications and expertise on paper, it is also important to have a personal connection, so select someone you can like, work with, and respect.

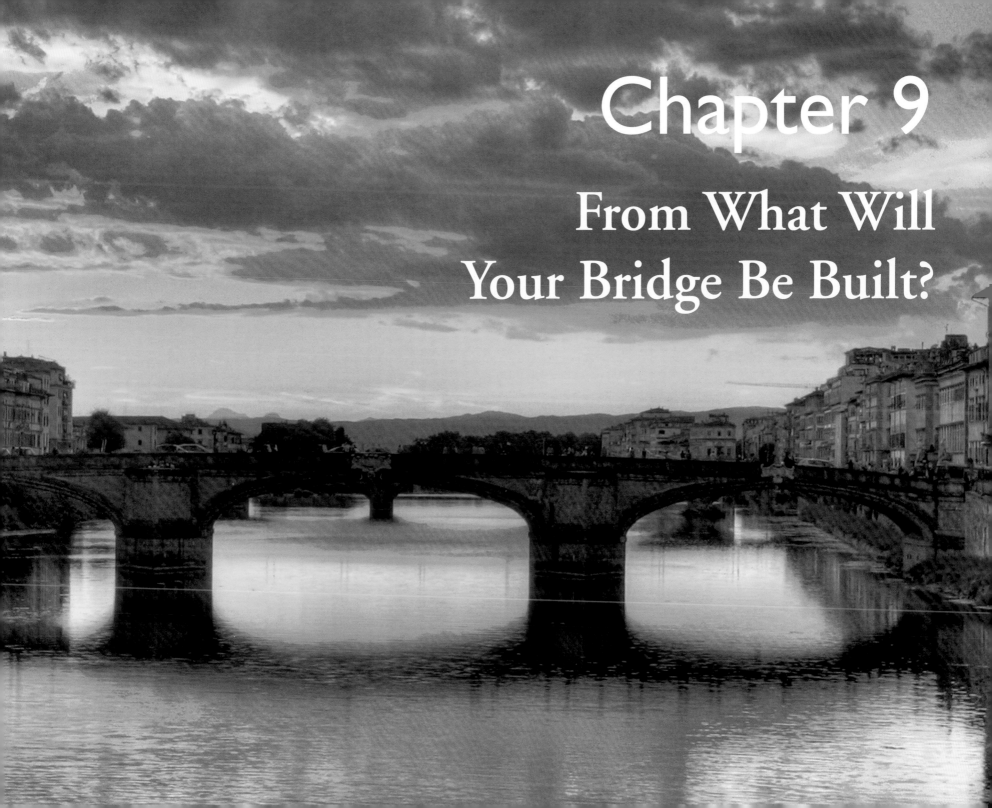

Chapter 9

From What Will Your Bridge Be Built?

What elements are appropriate for *your* financial foundation? How do you determine an appropriate allocation of assets? What mix of investments will you need now? In ten years? In twenty years?

The best bridge to your financial future will be built from the right mix of materials, products, and advice.

Asset Allocation, Diversification, and Rebalancing

Even if you are new to investing, you may already know some of the most fundamental principles of sound investing. How did you learn them? If you are like most people, you have learned them through ordinary, real-life experiences that have nothing to do with the stock market.

For example, have you ever noticed how some stores or boutiques often sell seemingly unrelated products, such as light bulbs and shoe pol-

An investor with a longer window of opportunity may feel more comfortable taking on a riskier or more volatile investment.

ish? At first glance, that may seem odd. After all, when would someone buy both of these items at the same time? Probably not very often if at all, but at different times, people will need both. By selling both items—in other words, by diversifying their product line—these stores can reduce the risk of losing money on any given day while providing the services and products their long-time customers need. If that makes sense, you can begin to understand asset allocation and diversification.

Asset Allocation: A Personal Decision

Asset allocation is the process of dividing an investment portfolio among different asset categories, such as stocks, bonds, and cash. Determining which mix of assets to hold in your portfolio is a very personal one. The asset allocation that works best for you at any given point in your life will depend largely on your time horizon and your ability to tolerate risk. It is advisable to have your advisor help you understand what each asset will likely mean to you at any given point in your life or career.

What Is Your Window of Opportunity?

Your window of opportunity is the expected number of months, years, or decades you will be investing to achieve a particular financial goal. An investor with a longer window may feel more comfortable taking on a riskier or more volatile investment because he or she can wait out slow economic cycles and the inevitable ups and downs of financial markets. By contrast, if you are saving up for a teenager's college education, you should take on less risk because you have a shorter window.

How Much Risk Can You Tolerate?

Risk tolerance involves just that—risk. It is your ability and willingness to lose some or all of your original investment in exchange for greater potential returns. If you are an aggressive investor with a high risk tolerance, you are more likely to risk losing money in order to get better results. If you are a conservative investor with a low risk tolerance, you will probably tend to favor investments that preserve your original investment. Your own risk tolerance levels depend upon multiple factors—long-term goals, length of time before you retire, ability to tolerate losses, and others.

Risk Versus Reward

When it comes to investing, risk and reward are inextricably linked. The phrase "no pain, no gain" perfectly sums up the relationship between risk and reward. Now, there is really no such thing as an investment without risk. Anyone telling you otherwise is doing you a disservice, because all investments involve some degree of risk. A prime example is securities, such as stocks, bonds, or mutual funds. It is important that you understand before you invest that you could lose some or all of your money if you invest in these kinds of investments. Again, an advisor can help

There is no such thing as an investment without risk.

you understand your risk. The lure of taking on risk, of course, is the potential for a greater investment return. If you have a financial goal with a long-time horizon, you are likely to make more money by carefully investing in asset categories with greater risk, like stocks or bonds, rather than restricting your investments to assets with less risk, like cash equivalents. On the other hand, investing solely in cash investments may be appropriate for short-term financial goals. With the thousands of options available at any given time, an advisor who is informed and up to speed is your best option for making intelligent and timely decisions.

Investment Choices

Anyone who has attempted to make his or her own investment decisions rapidly comes to understand that an overwhelming number of investment products exist. In fact, it is nearly impossible for the average investor to make informed investment decisions due to the sheer number of options available—stocks and stock mutual funds, corporate and municipal bonds, bond mutual funds, lifecycle funds, exchange-traded funds, money market funds, U.S. Treasury securities—which if any of these is right? Even if they are right today, will they be right next week? Next month? Next year? For many investors, investing in a mix of stocks, bonds, and cash can be a good strategy. Let us consider the characteristics of these three major asset categories:

Investing in a mix of stocks, bonds, and cash can be a good strategy.

Stocks

Stocks have historically had the greatest risk and highest returns among the three major asset categories. Most investors tend to load up on stocks because they frequently offer the greatest potential for growth. Stocks can rise meteorically, but they also can bottom out quickly. As a result, the volatility of stocks often makes them a very risky investment in the short-term. For example: large company stocks as a group have lost money on average about one out of every three years; sometimes the losses are quite dramatic. Investors that have been willing to hang onto the volatile returns of stocks over long periods of time generally have been rewarded with strong positive returns—unless the economy hits a period like we saw in 2008.

Bonds

Bonds are usually less volatile than stocks but sometimes offer less robust returns. If you are an investor approaching a specific financial goal, you might increase your bond holdings relative to your stock holdings because the reduced risk of holding more bonds might be attractive to you in spite of the lower potential for growth. Of course, some categories of bonds offer high returns similar to stocks. What you have to understand is that these bonds, sometimes known as high-yield bonds, also carry higher risk.

Cash

Among the safest investments are cash and cash equivalent investments—savings deposits, certificates of deposit, treasury bills, money market deposit accounts, money market funds, etc. The caveat is that they usually offer the lowest return of the three major asset categories. The good news is that your chances of losing money on an investment in this asset category are generally very low. Also, the federal government guarantees many investments in cash equivalents. Investment losses in nonguaranteed cash equivalents do happen, but not very often. The biggest concern for investors choosing to invest in cash equivalents is inflation risk (in other words, the risk that inflation will outpace and erode your investment returns as time passes).

Stocks, bonds, and cash are the asset categories most investors think of when investing for a retirement savings program or a college savings plan. Other asset categories exist—real estate, precious metals, commodities, private equity, and others. If you think you may want to include these asset categories within your portfolio, you need to understand that these asset categories usually have specific risks associated with their particular category. Before you make any investment decision in these categories, you should understand the risks of the investment and make sure the risks are appropriate for you.

> The three major asset categories have historically not moved up and down at the same time.

Why Asset Allocation Is Very Important

By including asset categories with returns that fluctuate up and down under different market conditions within a portfolio, an investor can help protect against significant losses. For example, the returns of the three major asset categories have historically not moved up and down at the same time. Market conditions that cause one asset category to do well often cause another asset category to have weaker returns. By intelligently investing in more than one asset category, you will reduce the risk that you will lose money, and your portfolio overall will enjoy a smoother ride. If one asset category's investment return falls, you will be in a position to counteract your losses in that category with better returns in another category.

The Art and Science of Diversification

The practice of spreading money among different investments to reduce risk is called diversification. By picking the right group of investments, investors can limit losses and reduce the fluctuations of investment returns without sacrificing too much of their potential gain. Bottom line, asset allocation is very important because it has a major impact on whether you will meet your financial goals. If you do not include enough risk in your investment portfolio, your returns may not be large enough to meet your goals. If you include too much risk in your portfolio, the money for your goals may not be there when you need it. Diversification is determined

almost entirely by your goals, the time you have to reach those goals, and how much—if any—potential risk will affect those goals.

Determining Your Asset Allocation Mix

Asset allocation mix is a complicated thing to determine because you are trying to pick a mix of assets with the highest probability of meeting your goals while doing so at a level of risk with which you can live. Here is the tricky part: the closer you get to meeting your goals, the more you will need to periodically adjust your mix of assets.

There is no single asset allocation model that is right for every investor or every financial goal. You will need to choose which is right for you. Now, if you thoroughly understand your time horizon and risk tolerance—and if you have some investing experience with a track record for consistent success—you may feel comfortable building your own asset allocation model.

If you choose to do this yourself, make sure you are up to the task. Many financial experts believe that determining your asset allocation is the most important decision that you will make regarding your investments. Many experts believe, in fact, that it is even more important than the individual investments you choose to buy. With that in mind, you will probably want to consider asking a financial professional to help you determine your initial asset allocation and then, at regular intervals, suggest adjustments for the future. As I mentioned earlier in this book though, be sure to do a thorough check of credentials, capabilities, and

There is no single asset allocation model that is right for every investor or every financial goal.

Diversification:
not putting all your eggs
in one basket.

disciplinary history before you hire anyone to help you with these critically important decisions.

The Difference between Asset Allocation and Diversification

Diversification simply means not putting all your eggs in one basket. This is accomplished by spreading your money among various investments in the hope that if one investment loses money, the other investments will make up for those losses. Whether your portfolio is adequately diversified will depend on how effectively you spread the money in your portfolio among different types of investments.

Diversification at Two Levels

Some investors struggle with knowing how to diversify their portfolio at two levels: between asset categories and within asset categories. Meaning, in addition to allocating investments among stocks, bonds, cash equivalents, and other categories, you will need to spread out your investments within each of those asset categories. The key is identifying investments in segments of each asset category that may perform differently under different market conditions.

Some investors attempt to do this by hoping to identify and invest in a wide range of companies and industry sectors. It is not that easy though, because the stock portion of your investment portfolio will not

be diversified, for example, if you choose to invest in only a handful of individual stocks. You will need many carefully selected individual stocks to be truly diversified.

Individual investors sometimes find it easier to diversify within each asset category through mutual funds rather than through individual investments from each asset category. Mutual funds are companies that pool money from many investors and invest in stocks, bonds, and other financial instruments. By doing this, mutual funds make it easier for investors to own a small portion of many investments.

This can create a false sense of security for investors, though, because a mutual fund investment does not necessarily provide instant diversification, especially if the fund focuses on only one particular industry sector. So if you invest in narrowly focused mutual funds, you may need to invest in more than one mutual fund to get the diversification you need. Within specific asset categories, that may mean investing in large company stock funds as well as some small company and international stock funds. Between all asset categories, that could mean considering stock funds, bond funds, and money market funds. The tricky part is that as you add more investments to your portfolio, you will often pay additional fees and expenses that will lower your investment returns. Make sure you consider these costs when deciding the best way to diversify your portfolio. If you get confused—which can happen easily—do not despair. These kinds of decisions are why investment advisors exist!

Mutual funds make it easier for investors to own a small portion of many investments.

Options for One-Stop Shopping:
Life Cycle Funds

Mutual fund companies know that investors are sometimes confused or frustrated by the endless choices. To accommodate investors who prefer to use one investment to save for a particular investment goal, such as retirement, some mutual fund companies have begun offering products known as "life cycle funds." These are diversified mutual funds that automatically shift towards a more conservative mix of investments. A life cycle fund investor picks a fund with the right target date based on his or her particular investment goal. The managers of the fund then will make all decisions about asset allocation, diversification, and rebalancing. It is usually easy to identify a life cycle fund because its name will likely refer to its target date. For example, you might see life cycle funds with names like "Portfolio 2010," "Retirement Portfolio 2020," or "Key Fund 2040."

Reasons for Changing Your Asset Allocation

The most common reason for changing asset allocation is a change in the timing of your window of opportunity. For instance, as you get closer to your investment date, you will probably need to change your asset allocation. Following that line of thought, most people investing for retirement hold less stock but have more bonds and cash equivalents as they get closer to retirement age. Other reasons to change your asset

As you get closer to your retirement date, you will probably need to change your asset allocation.

allocation would be a change in your risk tolerance, your financial situation, or any of your financial goals.

When Not to Change Asset Allocation

Smarter investors typically do not "chase the market." In other words, they do not change their asset allocation based on the immediate past performance of asset categories. For example, you would not want to increase the proportion of stocks in your portfolio when the stock market is hot. This is the kind of logic behind rebalancing your portfolio.

What Is Rebalancing?

One mistake investors make relatively frequently is failing to rebalance often enough. Rebalancing is when you bring your portfolio back to its original asset allocation mix. This is very necessary now and then because, over time, some of your investments often get out of alignment with your investment goals. How does this happen? Well, for instance, some of your investments will inevitably grow faster than others. By rebalancing, you will ensure that your portfolio does not overemphasize one or more asset categories, and you will return your portfolio to a comfortable level of balance and risk.

Here is an example: let us say your plan calls for stock investments to represent 60 percent of your portfolio. A stock market increase boosts your percentage of stock investments to 80 percent of your portfolio. In

Smart investors do not chase the market.

this case, you will want to either sell some of your stock investments or purchase investments from an under-represented asset category in order to reestablish your original asset allocation mix or balance.

Remember that when you rebalance, you will also want to review specific investments within each asset allocation category. If any of these investments are not in alignment with your investment goals, you will need to make changes to your asset mix to get back to your original allocation percentages.

While it is not as difficult as it sounds, it does require specific knowledge of all available investment options in these categories. Here are the three different basic ways you can rebalance your portfolio:

- You can sell off investments from over-represented asset categories, using the proceeds to purchase investments for under-represented asset categories.
- Add new investments to under-represented asset categories.
- If you are making regular contributions to your portfolio, you can make sure your investments go to under-represented asset categories until your portfolio is back into balance.

Before you rebalance your portfolio, your financial advisor can advise you regarding whether the method of rebalancing you choose will trigger transaction fees or tax consequences, and he or she can help you identify ways to minimize these potential costs.

Remember that when you rebalance, you will also want to review specific investments

When to Consider Rebalancing

Some investors balance their portfolio based on the calendar, while others do it based on their specific investments. Most financial experts recommend that investors rebalance their portfolios on a regular time interval, such as every six months or twelve months. The advantage of this "calendar" method is that the calendar offers a reminder of when you should consider rebalancing. Some advisors recommend rebalancing only when the relative weight of an asset class increases or decreases more than a certain percentage that you have identified in advance. The advantage of this method is that your investments tell you when to rebalance. In either case, rebalancing tends to work best when done consistently.

Where to Get Help

Rebalancing is something that most investors are not prepared to do by themselves. In the U.S. alone, there are more than ten thousand different mutual funds to choose from, for instance. Throw in the assortment of international funds, plus the natural fluctuations in national and international economic conditions, and making the best choices becomes even more difficult without the guidance of an experienced professional. The biggest reason to work with an advisor is that professional advisors have access to specialized research, comprehensive performance data, experience, and other tools to assist in helping you achieve your financial goals.

In the U.S. alone, there are more than ten thousand different mutual funds to choose from.

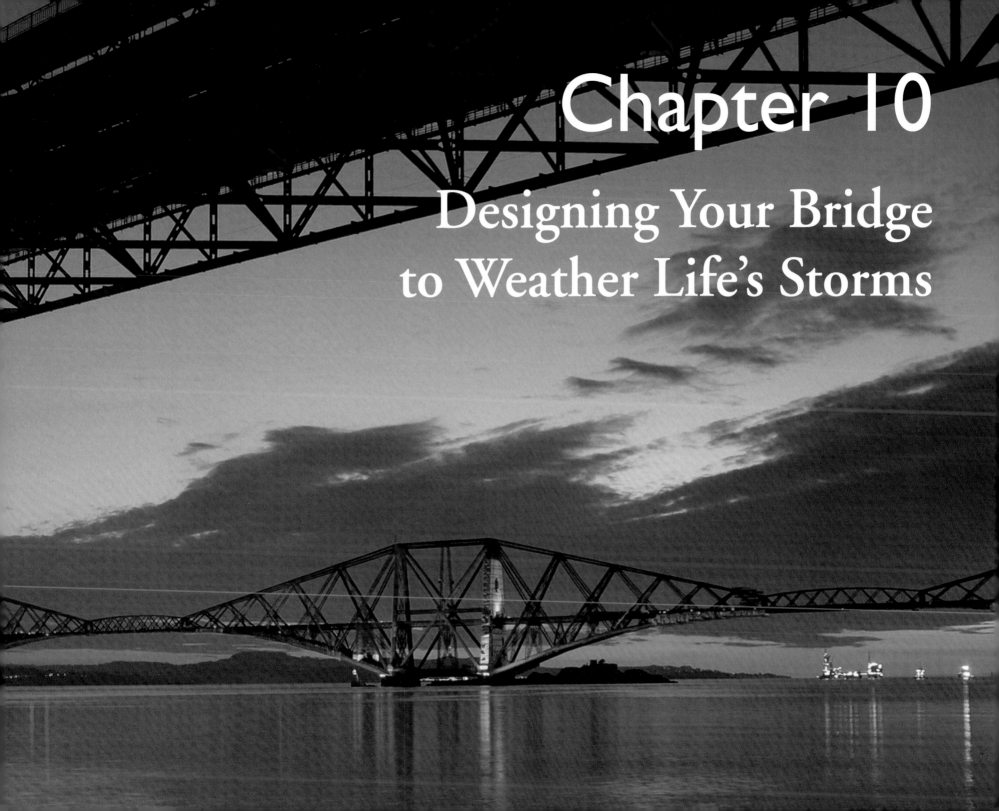

Chapter 10

Designing Your Bridge to Weather Life's Storms

It is hard to anticipate the obstacles life throws at you. However, there are steps you can take to keep yourself financially sound when you have to deal with the death of a spouse.

Single

That is a description most people stop thinking about once they get married, but for a person recently divorced or widowed, it is an emotional—and financial— trauma that can arrive in an instant.

Becoming single means that you are suddenly a sole proprietor, when you have been accustomed to being in a partnership. Whether or not that partnership was a success or a failure, it had its own style, and that style was the result of two people sharing decisions. For someone suddenly thrust into being single, it often takes time to learn how to find your own way again.

Leave time to handle
life's other chores.

Death of a Spouse

The strain of an uncertain financial future caused by the death of a spouse can understandably be among life's biggest stresses, but there are steps you can take to lessen the stress.

Initially, you should try to leave your investments alone for at least three months. Investing, buying, or selling can be dangerous at this emotional time. This is especially true for those who have never really handled their own money because they can fall victim to an unsolicited onslaught of well-meaning but confusing advice and, in rare cases, unscrupulous advisors.

As soon as you are feeling better, start to plan your own financial future. An orderly approach is important. Handle the basics first and leave the tough life choices for last, when you have put some distance between yourself and the pain.

This is a great opportunity to start with a clean slate. Make sure you can identify every expense and every source of income. Stay the course with what is necessary or desirable; change what is not. If the bills were always paid on time, keep it up. Consider auto-pay options if you have not already done so. The goal is to leave time to handle life's other chores.

If you have worked with a financial advisor previously, he or she should be able to help you identify what did work and what did not work in prior investments. The most important task is record keeping.

Record keeping includes bills, outstanding balances, investments, and bank statements. Files must be kept up to date. It is important to keep track of your financial life. A computer can help tremendously.

Locate All of Your Important Documents

Whether you work with an advisor or not, you will want to make sure you always know where to find all of your important documents. Here are twenty documents you always need to be able to get your hands on at a moment's notice:

- Birth certificate
- Social Security card
- Life insurance polices
- Other insurance policies
- Stocks
- Bonds
- Mortgage documents
- Deeds
- Leases
- Your will
- Trust documents
- Pension, profit-sharing, retirement plans
- Cemetery deeds
- Employment contracts

This is a great opportunity to start with a clean slate.

You would not let
a well-meaning neighbor or
friend perform surgery on
you, no matter how much
you needed it.

- Partnership agreements
- Corporate buy-sell agreements
- Divorce or separation agreements
- Marriage contracts
- Marriage certificate
- Funeral arrangements

Take a Realistic Snapshot of Your Finances

Compare monthly income to monthly expenses based on your new circumstances. If there is a shortfall, create a budget. If there is a surplus, save what is feasible and realistic in a money market fund until you can create an investing strategy. The main thing to remember here is to be realistic. If possible, use a spreadsheet to compare your assets and liabilities for an accurate view of your situation.

Beware of Well-Meaning Friends

It is normal for friends to volunteer to help in a time of need or distress. Some may offer to help you organize and handle your finances. Remember, though, that you are going to want someone with some knowledge or expertise. You would not let a well-meaning neighbor or friend perform surgery on you, no matter how much you needed it. Allowing someone unqualified to handle your finances, even if he or she means well, could potentially do just as much harm. So, it is okay to have someone else balance your checkbook, but make sure you stay on top of what is in your finances. Determine a manageable procedure to pay bills, make deposits and withdrawals, pay taxes, etc.

Make Sure You Understand Your Personal Credit Situation

This is simple to do. Get copies of your credit report and make sure you clean up any errors in the reports. If an ex-spouse had credit problems, write a brief letter of explanation to the reporting agency, as allowed under the federal Fair Credit Reporting Act, and tell them your situation. Explain your hardship and help them understand that the credit problem was not caused by you.

Take Care of Property Titles

If you are divorced, there was probably a distribution of property made either by agreement or ordered by the court. Either way, it should be clear who now owns the home, the accounts, and other assets. Similarly, if you are widowed, a will may have made ownership clear. If you have been working with a financial advisor, he or she will have helped you plan the inheritance together. You will be responsible for making changes to deeds, brokerage accounts, insurance, and other securities. Gather the pertinent documents, systematically contact all the institutions and custodians of accounts, and get the paperwork they require

to transfer title. Any qualified financial advisor can help you with these important and necessary tasks.

Set Your Individual Goals

These tasks may seem a little administrative and perhaps even bureaucratic, but these tasks will help you understand how much you spend, how much you receive, how much you own, and how much you owe. Once you fully understand these things, you will be prepared to make knowledgeable financial and lifestyle decisions for the rest of your life. For instance, do you want to move? Go back to school? Retire? Travel? Once you have this information at your fingerprints, you can set your own financial goals.

Rethink Your Need for Insurance

An often-neglected matter for someone who finds himself or herself suddenly single is how much and what type of insurance you should have. You may have too much, or you may want to change beneficiaries. If you are now the sole supporter of a child, you will likely want to increase the amount of life insurance you carry. If you support yourself by working, it will be important that you check out disability policies. They might represent the only way to remain independent if you cannot work.

Do you want to move?
Go back to school?
Retire? Travel?

Consider Professional Help from a Trusted Financial Advisor

Once you are sure you can cope with it all alone, think again. Financial advisors can sometimes find issues and help you achieve your goals in a more systematic approach than you can by yourself. A financial advisor can be your best friend, especially when you find yourself suddenly alone.

A financial advisor can be your best friend, especially when you find yourself suddenly alone.

Divorce Changes Everything

Anyone who has been through a divorce knows this is a true statement. Going through a divorce can be very difficult and stressful. Regardless of the reasons for the divorce, most people are overwhelmed with emotions and eager to move on as quickly as possible. However, there are important decisions to make in regards to finances, so it is very important that you proceed carefully and plan appropriately.

Hire a Professional

In a divorce, you are faced with giving up ownership of property, assets, investments, and debt. It is very important that this is done so that both parties emerge with equitable shares. This is not a situation where it is advisable to go through this on your own. Regardless of the size or complexity of your estate, you will want specialized attorneys assisting you in getting what is rightfully yours.

Prepare for the Settlement

A competent advisor can help you create a comprehensive list of assets and, more importantly, determine their value. A professional advisor will help you thoroughly understand the risks and potential tax consequences of retaining or giving up certain assets. Additionally, your financial advisor will help you and your attorney prepare for your settlement meeting. And although you will come to the settlement with a list of what you want, you are not likely to get everything. By being prepared to negotiate and give up some things in return for others, and by understanding the real, long-term value of the items you are discussing, you will be less likely to make a decision that you will regret later.

You Have to Protect Your Credit

If divorce appears inevitable, it is important to take action as soon as possible to protect your credit. Your advisor can help you obtain a credit report and properly evaluate it to determine any issues that need to be addressed. In the case of a divorce, it is important that you ensure there are no errors and identify any new sources of credit your spouse may have opened recently or without your knowledge. If you have or had joint credit accounts, you will want to consider removing either your name or your spouse's name if possible. This can prevent problems like having your spouse charge items against a joint account, or learning too late that your spouse has been missing payments, excessively charging, or otherwise causing a negative impact on your credit score.

Consider All Implications of a Divorce

If you have been part of a two-income couple, there are many things to consider prior to, during, and after a divorce. If possible, it is almost always preferable to review before going through with the divorce.

You will have to think through several lifestyle-related issues. For instance, how will your standard of living be affected after the divorce? How will your income and expenses match up? It is important to understand this clearly and thoroughly because this will affect what you can afford or what action you may need to take once the divorce is final.

Finally, you will want to examine any insurance benefits that may have been provided through your spouse's employer. If you were relying on coverage through their plan, find out if your employer offers benefits or what it might cost for you to purchase an individual policy.

Should You Have an Emergency or Contingency Fund?

Without a doubt, yes, you should.

Sooner or later, most of us face a crisis of some kind. The last thing you want to worry about at such a time is money, so it pays to be prepared financially for uncertainty or stressful times.

How will your income and expenses match up?

The emergency can be of any kind but is almost always the type you do not see coming: a medical emergency requiring surgery for a family member; an accident, which can force you to take leave extended without pay; an unexpected job loss, meaning you need money until you find another job; and so on.

Knowing that you have a fund you can use as an emergency or contingency fund provides financial stability and a peace of mind so that you can focus fully on problems as they arrive without worrying how you will handle immediate financial needs.

Knowing that you have a fund you can use as an emergency or contingency fund provides financial stability.

Setting Up an Emergency or Contingency Fund

The single most important feature of any emergency or contingency fund is liquidity—the ability to reach and use those funds when necessary. Since this money is earmarked for an unexpected issue, you will most likely need it at short notice. This money must be invested in highly liquid assets—a place where you can get back your money without any delay. Of course, it will be even better if you can also get a good rate of interest on this money.

How Should You Save for an Emergency or Contingency Fund?

There are some typical approaches that work well:

> The single most important feature of any emergency or contingency fund is liquidity.

Savings Account

Since liquidity is the single biggest criteria, the first option is to keep it in a savings account. It is the most liquid investment avenue, but it may give you a very low interest rate. Certificates of deposit and money market accounts are also great options and may provide significantly higher rates than savings accounts with close to the same liquidity.

Hybrid Account/Auto-Sweep

Some experts view this as a solid option for investing emergency or contingency fund money. These accounts provide the liquidity of a savings account, and at the same time, they provide the higher interest rates of CDs and money market accounts. A hybrid account or an account with an auto-sweep facility is an option that will help you keep your safety funds invested properly and earning a good rate of return.

How Much Should You Save for Your Emergency Fund?

That is a hard question to answer because it depends on your comfort level. It is whatever amount of money would make you feel safe and provide you with peace of mind during stressful times; only you can really decide how much is enough for you. However, having said that, a contingency fund should be at least six months of your income.

Is It Easy to Save an Amount This Large?

Not really. It would be an easy solution if you have received some lump-sum money as a dividend or bonus. That would allow you to create your fund in one easy step. You also can create your emergency fund over time from regular savings, even if you are not getting any large amount or bonus in the near future. Your financial advisor can help you budget for this.

So what are you waiting for? Save up for a contingency fund, have one thing less to worry about during your emergencies, and sleep better at night.

A contingency fund should be at least six months of your income.

Chapter 11
Maintaining and Protecting Your Bridge

When it comes to your financial future and your long-term financial plan, a little maintenance goes a long way. Here is how to track progress, manage change, and make the adjustments you will need to reach your long-term financial goals.

Maintenance and Repair

We've all seen the sad result of once-majestic bridges that have fallen into disrepair and are no longer functional. They may have been built well, but without ongoing maintenance and repair, they were destined to fail.

Likewise, a financial plan's safety and functionality must be reviewed, analyzed, and updated on an ongoing basis. Has something changed to cause the demands on it to exceed the limits of the original

plan? Are its safety requirements still in place and adequate to provide the necessary protection?

You have spent your life saving for retirement, and now that you are here, you are probably wondering what to do with your retirement savings. Most likely, your retirement nest egg is a combination of pension, IRA, and/or 401(k) accounts. You probably also have monthly income from Social Security and possibly from a part-time job or hobby. How do you manage both the money you have saved and the money that is coming in and build a retirement strategy that will see you through your remaining years?

The first thing to understand is that investing after retirement is frequently different from investing for retirement. The two guiding principles of investing after retirement are:

- Maintain a low risk
- Have a plan for drawing out funds

For some recently retired investors, it may be tempting to take the large sum of money in your retirement accounts and use it to invest in risky investments that promise high yield in a short amount of time. This is usually not a wise move though, since these types of investments can also have a high probability of losing money at any given time. Instead, you should look for investment options that are relatively stable. These accounts will likely have lower annual rates of return, but they can be much more secure and will keep your principal balance safer. If your

It may be tempting to take the large sum of money in your retirement accounts and use it to invest in risky investments that promise a high yield in a short amount of time. This is usually not a wise move.

> When planning for safety, remember: return of principal is as important as return on principal.

primary concern is maintaining the principal balance, choosing an account that is guaranteed by the Federal Reserve, such as CDs and money market accounts, is one way to go.

Use funds in a tax-intelligent way. The idea here is to lower your tax liability. This strategy allows you to maintain your principal balance. The less taxes taken out of your withdrawals, the more of your principal balance you will have to meet your everyday expenses. Also, take into account how much money you have coming in from sources such as Social Security, pensions, and annuities, and determine how much you will need to withdraw on a regular basis to meet your expenses. Remember that you will want to first withdraw money from any nonretirement savings accounts that you have in most cases. The good news is that since you have already paid taxes on these funds, withdrawals will not penalize you.

Once nonretirement funds are depleted, the next money sources should be your IRA and 401(k). One approach is to roll over your IRA and 401(k) into an annuity that pays a monthly guaranteed income. If you have funds not needed for retirement, consider positioning the funds for the benefit of your heirs. Using this approach will help ensure that the funds are handled as you desire.

A true financial maintenance plan continually organizes all of the necessary components and updates them yearly. The maintenance phase of your plan should include:

> Leave those who
> come after you a safe path
> on which to follow in
> your footsteps.

- Continuing your safety fund.
- College planning and teaching children to be self-sufficient.
- Careful monitoring of the entire portfolio's performance.
- Careful evaluation and analysis of overall market conditions.
- Ongoing evaluation and analysis of invested assets in terms of overall balance and mix.
- Ensuring sufficient assets are in place to support the bridge throughout your lifetime.
- Estate planning, including your will and collateral materials (power of attorney, durable power of attorney, physician directive, guardianship documents).

Think of this much-needed annual step as providing directions to the maintenance and repair crew that ensures your bridge is safe for the next generation, allowing you to transfer the bridge to future users in the most efficient way possible. In other words, you are leaving those who come after you a safe path on which to follow in your footsteps.

Insurance Is for Everyone

Insurance is probably the most misunderstood option in any long-term financial plan. If you consider insurance logically, though, there really should be no confusion. We all—each of us—face risks in our daily lives. That is why it is important to have adequate protection—so that you and your loved ones do not face unnecessary risk, or worse, suffer heavy financial losses.

Insurance is all about protecting you and your family from the costs associated with many of life's risks. Part of creating a sound financial plan is making sure you have all the insurance coverage you need and that you actually need all the coverage you have. If you have any kind of insurance, and if you are like most people that buy it, it is a safe bet you have never actually read your insurance policies. If that is indeed the case, it would probably be a good idea to read them. If you do not understand anything you read, call your insurance agent (or the insurance company's customer service department) and ask someone to explain it.

Basic Questions to Ask

As you review each policy, ask yourself these questions:

- Do I actually need this policy?
- Is the coverage adequate for my situation? Have I kept my insurance current for my needs? For example, have you increased the replacement cost coverage on your house as the value of your home has risen?
- Am I getting the best value for the premium I am paying? Would I save money and still keep adequate coverage if I raised my deductible, which would lower my premium? Should I spend a little

It is a safe bet that you have never actually read your insurance policies.

time searching for the same coverage at a lower price with another insurance company?

- Are there gaps in my coverage? In other words, are there situations that could possibly occur but that my policy would not cover?

- Would I get a discount if I bought all of my policies from the same insurance company, assuming I could get coverage as good as or better than I have now?

- Does my current insurance agent understand my needs and provide good service?

- Is my life, health, and ability to earn an income properly covered?

- Have I properly planned for my care when I reach an age or condition where I cannot handle this? Do I need to insure this risk?

Is my life, health, and ability to earn an income properly covered?

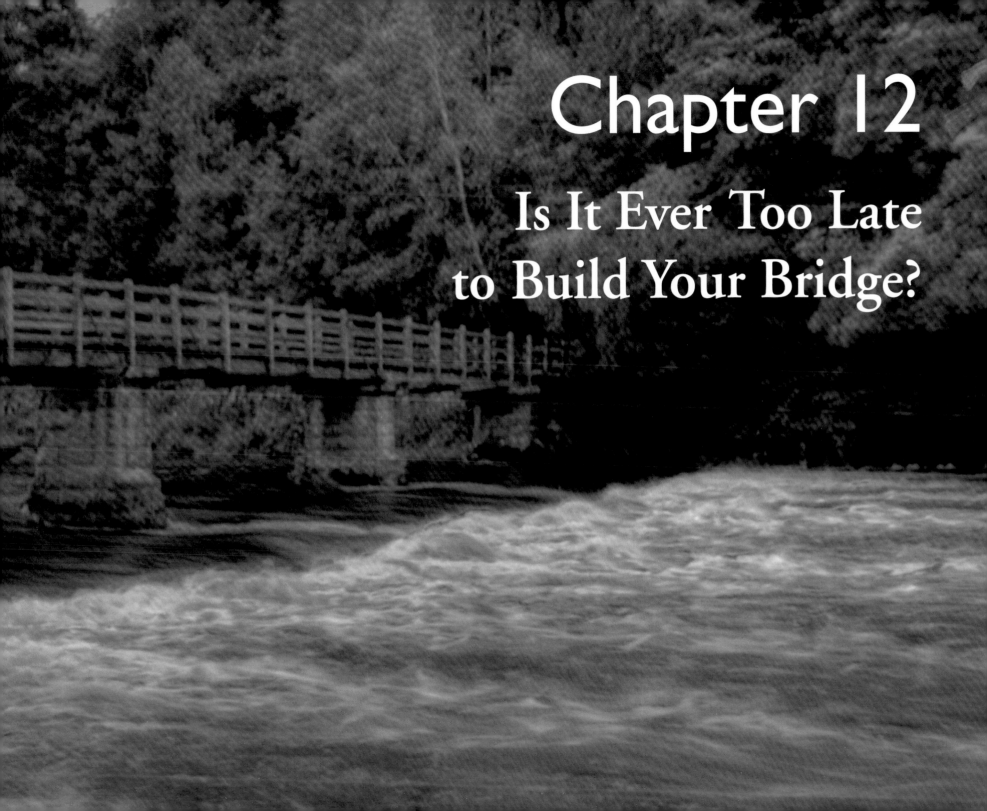

Chapter 12

Is It Ever Too Late to Build Your Bridge?

Regardless of age, there are accounts designed for retirement.

E arlier is better, but do not let anyone tell you it's too late. As the saying goes, "that dog won't hunt." Regardless of your age or financial condition, here is how to start planning today for the rest of your financial life.

How About You?

These days we often hear that people are not planning for retirement. All people understand that it is critical; all people understand they should do it. For many people though, it is one of those decisions that just keep getting pushed aside.

The good news is that no matter how late you start, it is better than not starting at all. Regardless (almost) of the age at which you start, there are special accounts designed to help you save for retirement. The

The compounding effect
of savings will build your nest
egg exponentially.

first step, no matter how late you start, is quantifying your goals. This involves accurately projecting income and expenses so you will know what you have to work with in building your financial future. Using these projections, you and your advisor will be able to establish the amount of time you realistically have to implement a plan, how much you can save and, more importantly, what rate of return is necessary from your investments to make sure that you achieve your goals in the time you have left. There is no question that it is better to start early, buy not planning at all will get you nowhere.

Regardless of when you start your financial plan, there are factors that you will want to take into consideration. A financial advisor can help you understand the myriad of factors that affect your planning. These factors can and will change based on your age at the time you start the plan and the amount of time you have to implement the plan. Additionally, these factors will not only help you understand where you are, but also at what pace you need to work. You need to carefully and thoroughly evaluate your personal circumstances; they will determine which types of investments are right for you. For instance, there are popular retirement accounts that include Individual Retirement Accounts (IRAs). There are also work-based plans, such as 401(k) accounts. Learning about and using these accounts will help you go a long way towards meeting your retirement goal.

Getting a Late Start in Planning

Your profile plan must take into account:

- Your age
- Where you are in your career
- Your need for liquidity
- Your current investment activity
- Your cash flow needs
- Your tax bracket
- The amount of return you require
- Your risk tolerance
- Your primary financial goals
- Ideal timing for reaching those goals

It Is Never Too Late

Do not put off planning for your future for another day. Start today; you will be glad you did.

Start today;
you will be glad you did.

Bridges

Not all of the bridges pictured in this book are identifiable. Some of the smaller bridges are from remote parts of the world and remain unknown. Other bridges could be identified by their location only, as they have never been given official names.

1–2: Tyne Bridge, England

8–9: Bay Bridge, San Francisco, California, USA

14: Brooklyn Bridge, New York, New York, USA

17: Ann W. Richards Congress Avenue Bridge, Austin, Texas, USA

18–19: Eilean Donan Castle Bridge, Scotland

27: Bronte Waterfalls, Haworth, England

30: Gapstow Bridge in summer, Central Park, New York, New York, USA

33: Bridge on Sligachan Isle of Skye, Scotland

34: Bridge over the River Nadiza, Slovenia

35: Bridge over Wahkeena Falls, Oregon, USA

38–39: Bridge over Lake Austin, Texas, USA

44: Golden Gate Bridge, San Francisco, California, USA

48–49: Pont des Arts Bridge, Paris, France.

57: Washington Street Bridge over Brandywine River, USA

58–59: Riga Railway Bridge, Riga, Latvia

69: Oberbaumbrücke Bridge, Berlin, Germany

72: Roman Aqueduct, Pont du Gard, France

84–85: Ponte Vecchio, Florence, Italy

86: Bridge in Limoges, Limousin, France.

100: Shelby Street Bridge, Nashville, Tennessee, USA

106: Navajo Bridge, Marble Canyon, Arizona, USA

120–121: Bigsby Bridge, Big Sur, California, USA

123: Eilean Donan Castle Bridge, Scotland

134: Bridge on Riverwalk, San Antonio, Texas, USA

140: High Five Interchange, Dallas, Texas, USA

142: Gapstow Bridge in winter, Central Park, New York, New York, USA

I hope that you found this book helpful and enjoyed the bridge photographs. For me, they symbolized the achievements in life's journey.

–Lloyd Lowe Sr.

About the Authors

Lloyd Lowe Sr. earned his Bachelor of Business Management from LeTourneau University and a Master of Financial Services with a concentration in Estate Planning from the University of Dallas.

In addition to his financial expertise and strong educational foundation, Lowe's background in business has provided him with a practical understanding of the balance that must be achieved to attain both short-term results and long-term financial wealth. He holds numerous professional licenses and certifications, including Certified Senior Advisor and Registered Financial Consultant. He maintains offices for his firm, LD Lowe Sr. Wealth Advisory, in Frisco, Dallas, and Arlington, Texas.

Ethan Bonar attended the University of Arkansas, where he earned his Bachelor of Science in Business Administration in Finance in 1999. After a short stay with Dean Witter in Plano, Texas, Ethan came to work with LD Lowe Sr. Wealth Advisory in 1999.

During his career in financial planning, Ethan has earned industry certifications such as Certified Senior Advisor and Registered Financial Consultant. As a senior partner and the Chief Compliance Officer at LD Lowe Sr. Financial Advisory, Ethan continues to serve his clients with comprehensive financial planning and investment management services. Ethan lives in Allen, Texas, with his wife, Julia, and their two young children, Reed and Aubrey.